DIGGERS AND PICKERS!

BEGIN YOUR DIG WHEREVER YOU ARE.

Adventure is only a rock away! Start by looking under your feet. Some rocks are easy to spot. Others are trickier to identify because they've been made into something else. Many are impossible to see because they're hidden deep inside the earth.

In this book and activity kit, you'll learn about different kinds of rocks, why some are striped or jagged or smooth, where to find them, and why they're important. And you'll get to practice what you learn by chipping away at the earthen block included in your kit!

Rocks come in every color, shape, and size. Many rocks are ancient, but some are younger than you.

Rocks go on adventures too. Some rocks that were once part of mountain peaks have traveled down to the bottom of the ocean.

Like a **geologist** who studies the earth, get ready to:

- EMBARK ON A MYSTERIOUS JOURNEY
- GRAB YOUR DIGGING TOOLS
- SEARCH FOR AMAZING BURIED TREASURE

C'MON, DIG IN FOR A ROCKIN' ADVENTURE!

DIG INTO EARTH'S LAYERS

WHAT LIES BENEATH?

Nearly 4,000 mi. (6,437 km) beneath your feet in the center of the earth is an inner core made of solid iron. Circling the core is a liquid-iron outer core. Surrounding the outer core are **pliable** rocky layers in the lower and upper mantles. These layers look like the inside of a giant jawbreaker.

The continental crust covers Earth's continents. In fact, you're standing on top of it right now! This crust is thick in some places and thin in others. It stretches across valleys and is sort of like the skeleton of mountains, made mostly of granite and basalt.

The oceanic crust is below the ocean floor and made of lava rocks.

Within the brittle crusts and reaching into the upper mantle is the **lithosphere**, made of plates. The plates are more like gigantic puzzle pieces than dinner plates. They sometimes scrape together or slide underneath one another and get crazy hot. This is known as the **theory** of plate **tectonics**. All that topsy-turvy action creates earthquakes, volcanic eruptions, and mountains.

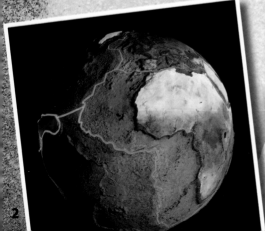

THE CRUSTY TRUTH

CRUST

UPPER MANTLE

OUTER CORE

INNER CORE

LOWER MANTLE

Around the upper mantle are two types of crust. This crust doesn't taste anything like pizza crust, but it's crunchy.

THE ROCK CYCLE

WEATHERING AND EROSION

PRESTO-CHANGO!

IGNEOUS

CRYSTALLIZATION

The rock cycle gets repeated again and again and again . . .

MAGMA

NEW ROCKS ARE FORMED EACH DAY, and existing rocks are always reinventing themselves. They transform from igneous to sedimentary to metamorphic in a process called the rock cycle.

TRANSPORT AND DEPOSITION

SEDIMENTATION

CEMENTATION

SEDIMENTARY

HEAT AND PRESSURE

METAMORPHIC

THREE OF A KIND

The rock cycle introduced you to three main types of rocks: igneous, sedimentary, and metamorphic. Let's dig deeper to find out even more!

IGNEOUS

Igneous rocks form as hot lava cools. The word igneous means "from fire." When **magma** gets trapped below Earth's surface and cools, instrusive igneous rocks are formed. When magma cools on top of Earth's surface, extrusive igneous rocks form.

You've likely seen granite, the most common type of igneous rock on Earth's surface. Cliffs are naturally made from granite. Many buildings and bridges are built from this stone because it's rock solid.

THE LONDON BRIDGE IS MADE OF GRANITE.

TYPES OF COMMON IGNEOUS ROCKS

- Basalt
- Granite
- Obsidian
- Pumice

SEDIMENTARY

Time, wind, extreme temperatures, and rainwater **erode** rocks. Gravity causes loose rocks from mountains to tumble down hillsides and drift along rivers. If rock particles are too heavy or get stuck behind other rocks, they stop moving. But some rocks keep moving. They grind and crash against other rocks and form smooth edges. Some rocks continue to break down and become grains of sand. Rivers transport sand all the way to oceans.

Clastic sedimentary rocks are formed when loose gravel, sand, silt, and clay pile up and get glued together.

Chemical sedimentary rocks are formed when water dissolves the minerals in rocks. The minerals mix with water and eventually get deposited somewhere else through **evaporation** and **precipitation**.

SEDIMENTARY ROCKS COVER 75 PERCENT OF EARTH'S SURFACE.

You've heard of organic food, but organic rocks? Organic sedimentary rocks such as coal often include compacted twigs, roots, and moss.
Organic rocks can also be made of shells, animal teeth, and dinosaur bones.

STALACTITES AND STALAGMITES IN CAVES ARE FORMED FROM THIS CHEMICAL SEDIMENTATION.

TYPES OF COMMON SEDIMENTARY ROCKS

- Coal
- Breccia
- Limestone
- Shale

METAMORPHIC

Metamorphic rocks are formed when igneous, sedimentary, and even metamorphic rocks experience pressure and heat deep within Earth's crusts. The rocks melt and the colors and textures change. Eventually, metamorphic rocks get pushed to Earth's surface.

I'M A CHANGED ROCK!

Michelangelo, a famous Italian sculptor, carved his statues from marble.

WHEN CALCIUM AND LIMESTONE COME TOGETHER, MUCH BIGGER CRYSTALS FORM AND MAKE SPECKLED PATTERNS IN MARBLE.

TYPES OF COMMON METAMORPHIC ROCKS

- Gneiss
- Marble
- Schist
- Slate

ROCKS ROCK THESE COOL FACTS

HOODOOS, SANDSTONE PILLARS IN BRYCE CANYON NATIONAL PARK, UTAH, LOOK LIKE THEY'RE FROM ANOTHER PLANET.

FLOATING ROCKS? PUMICE ROCKS FLOAT. THEY'RE POROUS—FILLED WITH LITTLE AIR POCKETS, LIKE A SPONGE.

THE WASHINGTON MONUMENT IS MADE OF MARBLE, GRANITE, AND BLUESTONE GNEISS.

Stone soup really exists. In Mexico, hot stones are used to heat soup in hollowed-out boulders. That's one colossal soup pot!

PLANTS BREAK APART ROCKS WHEN THEY GROW INSIDE A ROCK'S CRACK. OUCH!

EAT ROCKS? YOU BET! SALT IS A ROCK.

WHERE ON EARTH ARE THEY?

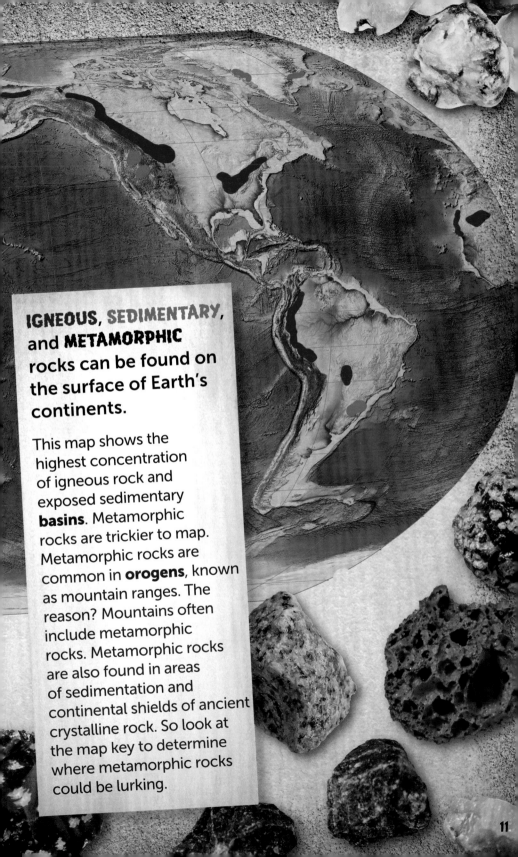

IGNEOUS, SEDIMENTARY, and METAMORPHIC rocks can be found on the surface of Earth's continents.

This map shows the highest concentration of igneous rock and exposed sedimentary **basins**. Metamorphic rocks are trickier to map. Metamorphic rocks are common in **orogens**, known as mountain ranges. The reason? Mountains often include metamorphic rocks. Metamorphic rocks are also found in areas of sedimentation and continental shields of ancient crystalline rock. So look at the map key to determine where metamorphic rocks could be lurking.

A ROCKY EXPERIMENT

IN THIS BOOK, YOU'VE READ HOW AND WHY ROCKS CHANGE. NOW YOU'LL SEE SEDIMENTATION IN ACTION.

Did you know pollutants are found in rainwater? Pollutants can come from factory or car **emissions**. This experiment will show rainwater impacts rocks in different ways.

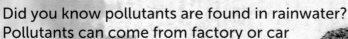

READY, SET, EXPERIMENT!

WHAT YOU NEED:

1. Five pieces of white chalk (represents rocks)- white chalk really works best!
2. Two clear plastic bottles with lids
3. Vinegar (represents rain)
4. Tablespoon

WHAT YOU DO:

1. Add 1 piece of chalk to a bottle.

2. Pour vinegar into the bottle until the chalk is submerged to represent a rock at the bottom of a calm lake.

3. Leave the mixture alone.

4. Meanwhile, add three pieces of chalk and 2 tablespoons of vinegar to the other bottle.

5. Tighten the lid. Shake the bottle for about 2 minutes to mimic rocks transported down a raging river.

6. Remove the chalk from the shaken bottle. Do you now have more than three pieces of chalk? What happened to the edges? How did the water change?

7. Remove the piece of chalk from the unshaken bottle and compare it to a dry piece of chalk. Do the pieces of chalk look different from each other? Does the water look any different?

Analyze: Which bottle of chalk dissolved faster and why? Think about how rainwater changes rocks in various ways.

Conclude: Do the results answer your initial question? You learned how sedimentation occurs at different rates, depending on the external forces.

TOOLS OF THE TRADE

GEOLOGISTS USE TOOLS TO UNEARTH EARTH'S MYSTERIES

Awesome tools are available for a rock hound like you. Geologists use tools interchangeably. Each tool is needed for a treasure hunt. Let's take a crack.

CHISEL

The pointed end of the chisel is used to pick at hard soil to reveal the mystery hiding. This tool is perfect for breaking up a specific area of soil. Use a chisel to carve away soil around a stone. A chisel can also be used like a shovel to dig or push aside soil. Chisels are usually made from wood or metal.

PICK, PICK, STRIKE IT RICH!

HAMMER

The head of a hammer is used to break apart packed down soil. The head of a hammer is made of metal, or sometimes wood. Gently tap the hammer against the soil to break up layers of rock.

Sometimes one tap is all it takes. Other times you'll need to keep on tapping. Even rocks have been used as hammers.

HAMMER TIME!

BRUSH

The brush is perfect to sweep away dirt to expose a possible buried treasure. A brush allows geologists to focus on delicate work and keep the dig surface free of **debris**. Like a hairbrush, a geologist's brush keeps everything neat.

It can look like a paintbrush or even a large hairbrush. Some geologists use paint-brushes bought from hardware stores.

SWEEP!

ROCK COLLECTION BAG

A bag is a handy way to store the rocks you find during and after your excavation.

MORE COOL TOOLS OF THE TRADE

- Goggles—protect eyes from flyaway rocks
- Notebook—write down your observations
- Magnifying glass—get a closer look at a rock **specimen**

DIG IT UP ACTIVITY

You never know what you'll discover until you start to dig. Get ready to excavate nine amazing rocks. Your one-of-a-kind rock kit includes an earthen block, hammer, chisel, and brush.

WHAT To Do:

1. Spread out newspaper or an old towel on a flat surface.

2. Tap the dirt block with the hammer to loosen hard dirt.

3. Position the tip of the chisel against the block and tap the end of the chisel with the hammer to break away a specific area of dirt.

4. Carve away dirt from around a rock with the chisel.

5. Brush and sweep away excess dust.

6. Wiggle the rock loose from the dirt.

7. Keep going until you excavate a total of nine rocks.

ADVENTURER TIP: WHENEVER YOU HEAD OUT ON AN EXCAVATION, GET PERMISSION BEFORE YOU BEGIN. SOME ROCKS ARE PROTECTED AND NOT ALLOWED TO BE REMOVED FROM CERTAIN SITES. NEVER ENTER A MINE OR CLIMB UNSAFE CLIFFS.

MAKE 'EM SHINE.

Clean rocks with a damp cloth. Allow your rocks to dry. Add a couple of drops of mineral or baby oil to your cloth and polish the rocks with the cloth until they dazzle.

YOU HIT THE MOTHER LODE!

WHAT DID YOU DIG UP?

GET TO KNOW YOUR ROCKS

You rock! You excavated some dynamite rocks. Your assortment includes a mix of igneous, sedimentary, and metamorphic rocks. Check out the incredible colors and crazy patterns. Feel the different textures.

HEY, WHAT'S YOUR NAME?

WHERE YA FROM?

PINK GRANITE

This crystallized igneous rock is pink granite. It is an intrusive igneous rock that formed below Earth's crust. First, your rock experienced tons of pressure and mega-hot temperatures. Then, it slowly cooled. Minerals got pressed together and created a grainy pattern. Do you see grains? This rock has been through a lot, and it's extra strong.

That's why pink granite is used to make kitchen counters and even buildings.

Pink granite is mined from a **quarry** in New Jersey. It can be found other places, such as Texas and even along the coast of France.

Fiery!

PUMICE

HOLEY ROCK FORMATIONS!

Pumice is igneous and formed outside Earth's crust. When a volcano erupted extra-thick lava, the gas couldn't escape. The lava turned into a frothy mixture with lots of air bubbles. When the froth cooled quickly, pumice formed. Did you notice how light your rock is? You would be able to lift a pumice boulder the size of a beach ball over your head because it's filled with air. Pumice is often used as a polishing agent and is sometimes an ingredient in toothpaste!

Can you guess where pumice stones are found? If you guessed around volcano eruption sites, you're correct. Pumice is found throughout the world wherever volcanoes are found.

SNOWFLAKE OBSIDIAN

This igneous gem is an extrusive stone, which means it formed on the outside of Earth. Your rock was created when volcanic lava cooled fast and partially crystallized. The result? Snowflake-patterned glass! Your rock contains the same minerals as granite. The main difference between snowflake obsidian and granite is linked to the cooling process. Remember what you learned about how your piece of pink granite slowly cooled?

Snowflake obsidian is found in North and South America.

VOLCANIC GLASS!

BRECCIA

This rock is a perfect example of how clastic sedimentation looks. Can you see all the little bits of rocks within this rock? All those pieces are stuck together. It's possible that breccia is made up of igneous, metamorphic, and even sedimentary rocks.

You can tell a lot about your rock by paying close attention to the texture. Do you remember how river rocks have smooth edges? Because of breccia's rough surface, we can tell it hasn't traveled downriver.

ROUGHIN' IT!

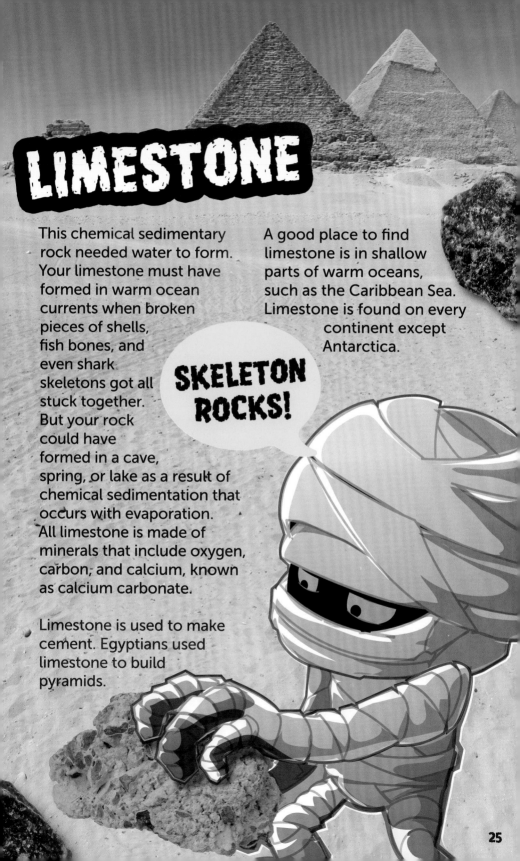

LIMESTONE

This chemical sedimentary rock needed water to form. Your limestone must have formed in warm ocean currents when broken pieces of shells, fish bones, and even shark skeletons got all stuck together. But your rock could have formed in a cave, spring, or lake as a result of chemical sedimentation that occurs with evaporation. All limestone is made of minerals that include oxygen, carbon, and calcium, known as calcium carbonate.

Limestone is used to make cement. Egyptians used limestone to build pyramids.

A good place to find limestone is in shallow parts of warm oceans, such as the Caribbean Sea. Limestone is found on every continent except Antarctica.

SKELETON ROCKS!

COAL

Coal is a sedimentary rock bursting with energy. Your rock is organic because it's made up of plants that were alive. Gravity, mud, and water pushed plants inside the earth where it's always steaming hot. Then the plants melted together at just the right temperature over long periods of time to form your piece of coal. Do you know what else?

The energy plants absorb from the sun shows up in coal. That's why coal can be used to make electricity. Here's an amazing factoid: It takes 10 ft. (3.1 m) of piled up dead plants to make a 1-ft. (30.5-cm)-thick piece of coal.

Where is coal found on our planet? Every single continent.

Electric!

GREEN SERPENTINE

Green serpentine is named after a snake because of its color. Iron gives the rock its color. Your rock formed deep within the oceanic crust when minerals became wet at low and cool pressures, making it metamorphic. Does your rock feel greasy? The mineral makeup is the reason it feels the way it does.

Green serpentine is found in the United States, China, England, Italy, New Zealand, Norway, and Russia. Rock hounds have found green serpentine—California's state rock—lying around in the California foothills .

HISS!

PHYLLITE

This metamorphic rock is phyllite. Check out the repeated **parallel** layers, known as foliation. The striped layers sometimes break apart. Your wrinkled rock is made of miniature minerals that stuck together when they heated up inside the earth's crust. This rock looks shiny because it cooked longer than other sedimentary rocks.

Phyllite is found around the world—even on Mount Everest!

EXTRA HOT!

RED MARBLE

Red marble is a non-foliated metamorphic rock. That's a scientific way to say you won't find layered patterns on this rock. Instead, you can see lots of crystals melted together. Your red marble formed when limestone experienced pressure and extreme heat within the earth. How cool is that? And limestone is made when broken pieces of shells, gravel, and algae get all stuck together. Red marble is an awesome example of the rock cycle in action.

Red granite shows up in lots of places, such as Argentina, Sweden, Egypt, and the United States.

MORPHED!

BAG 'EM AND TAG 'EM ACTIVITY

Green serpentine

ROCK DECODER

Draw a line from the picture of the rock to the description that matches it.

ROCK

Snowflake obsidian

Phyllite

Breccia

Red Marble

MYSTERY SOLVED!

ROCK DESCRIPTION

Shiny and layered

Formed from skeletons

Grainy patterns

Many types of rocks stuck together

Lots of holes

Looks like glass

Named after a snake

Crystals melted together

Compressed plants

Pumice

Limestone

Coal

Pink granite

GLOSSARY

analyze – to study and evaluate

basins – low-lying areas (prairies), surrounded by higher areas (mountains)

debris – the remains of anything broken down

emissions – chemicals passed into the atmosphere

erode – to wear away gradually

evaporation – water mist, vapor, or fog

geologist – a scientist who studies the earth

lithosphere – part of Earth's outer surface made of plates

magma – hot liquid below Earth's surface

orogens – mountains

parallel – layers of lines that never cross over the others

pliable – bendable

precipitation – moisture in the atmosphere such as rain, snow, or hail

quarry – open excavation pit

specimen – a sample of something

stalactites – icicle-like rocks that hang from cave roofs and are formed by drips of mineral-rich water

stalagmites – pillars on cave floors formed by drips of mineral-rich water

tectonics – the study of how the earth changes its form

theory – an idea that could explain something in nature